THE FIVE-MINUTE

SALAD

THE FIVE-MINUTE
SALAD

GAIL DUFF

Conceived and produced by Breslich & Foss, London

Photography by Mark French
Styling by Vicky Wood
Illustrations by Marilyn Leader
Designed by Clare Finlaison
Original design by Lisa Tai

Published by Crown Publishers, Inc., 201 East 50th Street
New York, New York 10022.
A member of the Crown Publishing Group.

CROWN is a trademark of Crown Publishers, Inc.

Manufactured in Singapore

Library of Congress Cataloging-in-Publication Data

Duff, Gail.
The five-minute salad / Gail Duff.
p.   cm.
1. Salads.   1. Title.
TX740.D84 1992
641.8'3—dc20   91–27148
                                          CIP

ISBN 0-517-58766-1

10 9 8 7 6 5 4 3 2 1

First American Edition

Contents

THE FIVE-MINUTE APPROACH

Salads, consisting mainly of raw ingredients, are the quickest of foods to prepare and, in five minutes, you can achieve a wonderful variety of flavor, texture, shape and color.

Salads are not just for hot summer days. They can make a tantalizing first course to wake up the taste buds before a hot main meal; they will always provide a refreshing contrast to rich main dishes, whether meat-based or vegetarian; and, with the addition of more substantial ingredients, such as cold meat, fish, beans or cheese, a salad can itself be the main meal. Salads do not even have to be cold. If the ingredients are quickly stir-fried in hot oil they will maintain a crisp, crunchy texture and raw flavor. The further addition of vinegar or lemon juice to the pan completes the salad character.

If you keep the number of ingredients fairly small and the dressings tasty but simple, all these different types of salad can be prepared in five minutes. They will look superb and taste wonderful and you will have plenty of time to spend on the other parts of your meal and also to enjoy eating them.

INGREDIENTS

Before looking in more detail at the ingredients that you can use to make salads in five minutes, it is worth mentioning the fact that, in order to work quickly, you must always make sure that you have your ingredients to hand. Although a certain amount of time is allowed in each recipe for a quick rinse of a lettuce or a carrot under a cold tap, there is no allowance for a hunt through the back of a cupboard for a jar of mustard that you thought you put there last year!

It is a good idea to have a 'special ingredients' cupboard into which you put all your vinegars, sauces, spices and flavorings, each in a separate section, so you know where to find them as soon as you open the cupboard door. This will not only help you to make salads in five minutes, it will save you time and trouble whatever you intend to cook.

VEGETABLES

In most salads, vegetables are the main ingredients and it is surprising just how many can be eaten raw.

The leafy vegetables are more traditionally associated with salads than any other type. In order to make each salad as different as possible, a wide variety of these have been used in the following recipes. They are quite interchangeable so, if one is unobtainable, use another.

In some cases, names for salad vegetables can vary, particularly in US and UK usage. The most dramatic example is the use of 'chicory' and 'endive'. The vegetable called chicory

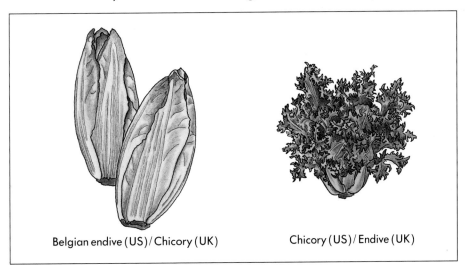

Belgian endive (US) / Chicory (UK)   Chicory (US) / Endive (UK)

in the US is called endive in the UK, whereas what is called chicory in the UK is called Belgian endive in the US. In this book, the US terms for chicory and endive are used. In other cases the UK term appears in parenthesis where applicable – e.g. scallions (salad onions).

All the leafy vegetables store well in the refrigerator and, to save time at the preparation stage, it helps if you wash them before you put them away. Hold them by the stalk end and give them a rinse under cold running water. Then shake them dry. Put them into a plastic box or bag and store them in the bottom of the refrigerator for up to three days. If you are using vegetables straight from the shopping bag, the same method of washing applies.

Lettuce, lollo rosso, chicory, and Belgian endive are constructed in similar ways, with their leaves all joined to the stem. To separate the leaves, simply cut across a short way above the stem. Discard the stem and the leaves should separate easily. If the leaves are still a little damp for your liking, place them quickly in a dry towel and pat them gently.

Radicchio and the much larger Chinese leaves are also joined at the stem but their leaves are more densely packed. To separate the leaves of radicchio, cut the whole vegetable in half downwards and cut away the stem from the center. It is easier to shred or chop Chinese leaves without separating the leaves. Cabbage, which is still more densely packed, should be cut into lengthwise quarters. The stems can then be cut out easily before the unseparated leaves are shredded.

The two types of cress, watercress and mustard and cress, need very little preparation. (Mustard and cress, seedlings grown and sold in a small box, is much used in the UK, although not in the US. Alfalfa sprouts are very similar and can be used in exactly the same way.) Keep watercress tied in a bunch for washing, holding the stems and placing the leaves under running water. Shake the bunch and, holding the stem end, chop as many of the leaves as you need. Mustard and cress needs no washing. Simply cut off the growing shoots with a sharp knife or kitchen scissors.

Chopping celery

1 *First cut lengthwise down center of stalks.*

2 *Holding several half-stalks together, cut crosswise into chunks all the way up the stems.*

To separate celery stalks, cut across the base of the head, removing the hard end. You should then find that the stalks separate easily. To wash them, hold them together by the tops of the stems and let the water run through them. If you buy unwashed celery, wash and separate the stems before storing. To chop celery, slice lengthwise down the center of the stalks with a sharp knife. Then, holding two stalks (i.e. four halves) together, chop quickly across with a sharp chopping knife.

Fennel is similar in construction to celery but prepared slightly differently. After you have cut across the base to remove the stalk you will find that the leaves will stay together. Cut the bulb into lengthwise quarters and thinly slice them, two quarters at a time. The leaves can be chopped and used as a herb.

Chopping fennel

1 *Hold the bulb on its side and cut across the base to remove the thick stalk part.*

2 *Cut down through the center.*

3 *Lay the half bulb flat on the cut surface and cut down through the center again. Thinly slice the quarters crosswise.*

Carrots should be grated for most salads. Again, setting up the food processor may take more time than it saves. You may prefer to lay a hand grater across the salad bowl and grate the carrot directly into the dressing.

Tomatoes simply need rinsing under cold water and drying in a towel. Use a serrated knife for slicing, either crosswise into rings or into lengthwise wedges.

Cucumbers do not need to be peeled, but it is a good idea to rinse them in cold water before slicing. Although food processors can cut cucumbers into even slices, a good cook with a large, sharp, chopping knife can be almost as quick. Also, by the time you have set up the food processor and found the appropriate blade, you may well have used up a large part of your five minutes.

Preparing a sweet pepper

1 *Insert the tip of a sharp knife near the stalk and cut round in a circle shown by the dotted line. The stem and most of the small pithy core can then be pulled away.*

2 *When the stalk has been removed, cut down through the center.*

3 *If there are any seeds or small pieces of pith on these ribs, trim them away with the point of the knife.*

4 *Slice lengthwise into strips and cut the strips into the required lengths.*

Red, green and yellow sweet peppers may look as though they are going to be time consuming but, with practice, even these can be prepared quickly. First, remove the cores by inserting the point of a sharp knife into the top of the stalk and running it round in a circle. Pull the stalk and out comes the core with it. Then slice the pepper in half lengthwise and slice away the long pithy parts (there are only about two) which hold the seeds. The pepper is then ready for slicing as needed.

Some of the recipes include canned vegetables and the only preparation they need is to be drained. To save fiddling about with colander and sieves, when you open the can do not remove the top completely but leave a join of about ½ inch (1.3 cm). Simply tip the can over the sink holding down the part of the lid opposite the join with your fingertips. The vegetable can then be used directly from the can.

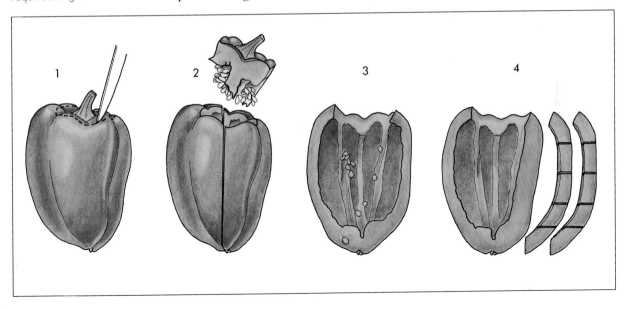

HERBS

The addition of herbs can make an ordinary salad taste very special. The herbs must, however, be fresh as dried ones will not have time in five minutes or less to soften in the dressing or to give out a good flavor.

Herbs are best when they are home-grown and freshly picked, but excellent fresh ones can also be bought from supermarkets and markets. Store these herbs in plastic bags in the bottom of the refrigerator for up to three days.

If your herbs are growing near the house or in pots or a window box, there may be just enough time within your five minutes for cutting them. If, however, you have to put on boots and make an expedition up the garden, you should allow extra time for this.

Chopping time, however, is allowed within the five minutes. The quickest and easiest way of chopping herbs is to use a flat chopping board and a large, heavy, sharp cook's knife. Lay the herbs on the board and begin by cutting them into lengths of about ½ inch (1.3 cm). Then gather the leaves together, hold an end of the knife blade in each hand and bang the knife repeatedly down on the herbs.

Chopping herbs

Place a pile of herbs on a board. Holding the blade of a large heavy knife in both hands, chop it up and down on the herbs, reforming the pile as you go. Continue until the herbs are uniformly chopped.

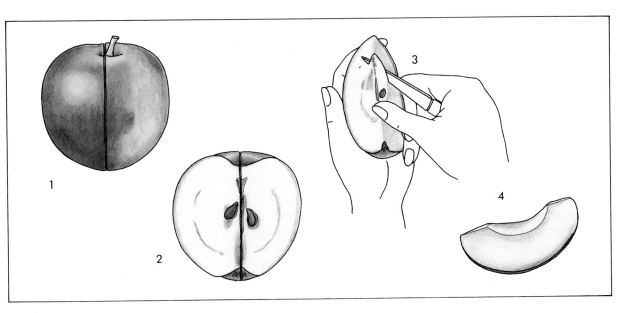

Slicing an apple

1 *Cut the apple in half lengthwise.*

2 *Cut each half lengthwise.*

3 *Holding the apple quarters in one hand, cut away the center part, removing the core and seeds. Slice the apple while holding it in the same way.*

4 *Apple slices will be shaped like this.*

FRUITS

Fruits liven up both the appearance and flavor of salads and there are also tricks to preparing these quickly so that you can keep within your five minutes.

To slice an apple, first cut it lengthwise into quarters. Then, holding each quarter in your hand, slice away the core part which is on the central point. Slice the quarter while still holding it in your hand.

Apricots and peaches can also be sliced in the hand rather than on the chopping board. Cut all round the groove in the fruit and pull the two halves apart. Take out the stem and slice the fruit. Apricots can be sliced directly into the salad bowl. A difficulty may arise with some peaches which have a pit or stone which clings to the flesh. In this case, cut the slices of peach from the pit or stone rather than removing it first.

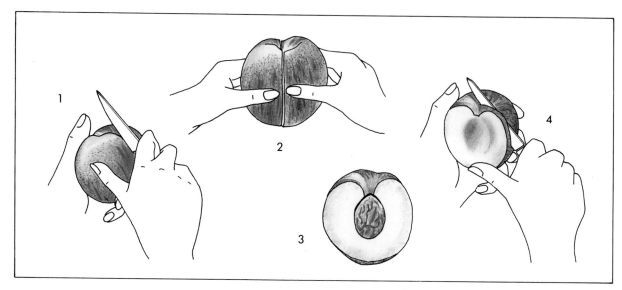

Slicing a peach

1 *Run the knife round the natural groove in the fruit.*

2 *Pull the two halves apart.*

3 *Pull out the pit.*

4 *Cut the pitted half into lengthwise slices.*

Apricots – *cut in the same way as peaches.*

COOKED INGREDIENTS

Some ingredients have to be cooked and cooled before being made into a salad. The following are used in the recipes in this book.

Ham: Buy ham that has been cut from the bone or cook your own. To cook a joint of ham, soak it first in cold water for four hours. Drain it, put it into a pan of fresh water together with a small carrot, a celery stick and an onion, all roughly chopped, a teaspoon each of black peppercorns and cloves, a bouquet garni and, if wished, a small glass of cider. Bring to the boil and simmer until tender. Lift out of the cooking liquid and cool.

Chicken breasts: To poach, put into a pan of water a carrot, celery stick and onion all roughly chopped, a bunch of herbs, a teaspoon of black peppercorns and a pinch of salt. Bring them to the boil. Add the chicken breasts and simmer gently for 20 minutes. To roast, dot the chicken with butter and wrap, together with a sprig of herbs, in buttered foil. Lay the parcel on a baking sheet and put it into a preheated 400°F/200°C/gas 6 oven for 25 minutes.

Sausages: These can be either fried, baked or grilled, according to taste.

Beans: Soak dried beans in cold water for at least four hours, drain them and put them into a saucepan with fresh water. Bring to the boil, make sure that they boil for 10 minutes and then simmer until tender. They may also be cooked in a pressure cooker in which case the soaking may be omitted. Cooked beans will keep in a covered container in the refrigerator for up to two days.

Rice: Put 8 oz (200 g) long grain brown rice into a saucepan with 20 fl oz (600 ml) cold water and ½ teaspoon salt. Bring to the boil, cover and simmer gently for 40 minutes or until the rice is tender and all the water absorbed. There is no need to wash rice cooked in this way. Tip it into a basin to cool. Keep in a covered container in the refrigerator for up to two days.

DRESSINGS
The most important part of a salad is its dressing. Well made, it will bind together a collection of unrelated flavors and textures into one whole dish rather than combatting parts.

Depending on the type of salad that you are making, the dressing is added at different times. If you are mixing a certain number of the ingredients in a bowl with the dressing, here is one quick tip: add the dressing first. This saves time transferring it from one bowl to another and will also save time on the washing up.

If the salad is to be served in one bowl, mix the dressing in the bowl first and then gently fold in the other ingredients. This ensures even coating with the dressing as well as being more convenient. Even if the dressed salad is to be transferred to a plate, dressing and salad can still be prepared first in one large bowl.

Basic Oil and Vinegar Dressing: This dressing is used throughout each recipe section. It can be made on the spot or bottled and kept in a cupboard for instant use. If you make a lot of salads, perhaps one every day or at least every other day, it is well worth making a large amount at a time. The simple formula is: two parts oil to one part vinegar. Pour into a bottle and shake well and always shake before use as the oil and vinegar separate when left standing. If you are making only enough for one salad, beat the ingredients well together with a spoon.

Oil: Olive oil is ideal for salads because of its fine flavor but grape seed oil or sunflower oil make good substitutes.

Vinegar: A good quality, light-colored and delicate-flavored white wine vinegar is the most universal. A light-colored cider vinegar can be used instead. Malt vinegar, except where specifically called for, is too harsh and strongly flavored.

Flavored vinegars: Lemon vinegar is mentioned in one recipe. To make this, wipe and chop one lemon, the peel and pith together with the flesh. Pour off a little from a full bottle of white wine vinegar and push in the lemon pieces. Leave the bottle in a warm place for two weeks, shaking it daily. Strain off the vinegar and it is ready for use.

Herb vinegars are made in the same way, using four herb sprigs instead of the pieces of lemon.

MAYONNAISE

Although you can buy mayonnaise, it never tastes as good as the homemade variety. You cannot include it in your five minutes preparation time so it must be made and stored in advance. It will keep for up to a week in a covered container in the refrigerator.

2 egg yolks
½ tsp mustard powder
freshly ground pepper, white if possible
8 fl oz (200 ml) olive, grape seed or sunflower oil
up to 2 Tbs white wine vinegar

Put the egg yolks into a bowl with the mustard powder and pepper and beat well. Drop by drop, beat in 2 tablespoons of the oil. Add 2 teaspoons of the vinegar, one at a time and beating well. Add the oil, slowly, about 2 teaspoons at a time and beating after each addition. If you are using an electric beater, the oil can be added in a steady stream. When all the oil has been added and the mayonnaise is thick, taste it. Add as much more vinegar as you think necessary.

SERVING A SALAD

Mixtures of colorful ingredients glistening in a smooth dressing need little garnishing other than that called for in the recipe. They do, however, benefit from being served on or in attractive crockery. You will find in the following pages salads that are served on side plates, in individual bowls, in large salad bowls or on oval serving platters. Before you start timing your five minutes, spend one extra on selecting the right dish.

WHAT TO SERVE WITH A SALAD

If you are intending to make a salad in five minutes, then you are probably looking for something quick and easy to serve with it.

The first courses are best with some sort of bread: wholewheat bread with butter, warmed rolls, pita bread or hot toast are all suitable.

With a main course salad, you have a choice of hot potatoes, wholewheat bread, pita breads or salads of rice or pasta. Not all of these go with every salad. As a rough guide, baked potatoes or plainly boiled new potatoes are best with the meat, cheese or egg-based salads. Wholewheat bread goes best with seafood; pita breads go well with beans or nuts. Neither hot rice nor hot pasta are as good as hot potatoes when put with salads. In fact, rice and pasta are best cooked, cooled and made into salads themselves: rice to go with beans, nuts and meat, and pasta with cheese, beans and nuts.

Portions: All the following recipes are designed to serve four people.

1
SALADS TO
START A MEAL

HAM AND APPLE

Ingredients
2 Tbs olive oil
1 Tbs cider vinegar
2 tsp clear honey
2 tsp spiced granular
mustard
6 oz (150 g) lean ham
2 medium-sized cooking
apples or crisp dessert
apples such as Granny
Smiths

Mustard and apples are the traditional accompaniments to ham and pork, and honey is often used to coat them as they are roasting. Here, all the ingredients are combined to make individual small salads that have a sweet-and-savory flavor.

The salads work best with ham that has been cut thickly from the bone, but ordinary sliced ham may be used.

If you have a basic oil and vinegar mixture in the pantry (see page 16), use 3 tablespoons to add to the honey and mustard.

In a bowl, beat together the oil, vinegar, honey and mustard. Cut the ham into small pieces and fold it into the dressing. Wipe the apples but do not peel them. Cut them lengthwise into quarters and cut away the cores. Cut each quarter into thin slices. Put a portion of the ham salad into the center of each of four small plates and arrange the apple slices around the ham.

If the salads have to stand for a long time before serving, paint the apple slices with a little extra vinegar to prevent them from going brown.

1 *Beat together the oil, vinegar, honey and mustard and fold in the diced ham.*

2 *Quarter, core and slice the apples.*

3 *Put ham mixture into the center of four small plates and arrange apple slices around.*

FENNEL AND GARLIC SAUSAGE WITH HOT DRESSING

Ingredients
1 bulb fennel, about
 8 oz (200 g)
1 green pepper
4 oz (100 g) garlic
 sausage, bought thinly
 sliced
4 Tbs olive oil
1 garlic clove, crushed
2 Tbs white wine vinegar
1 tsp Dijon mustard
parsley sprigs for
 garnish, optional

Slices of fennel are sometimes served with a hot garlic dip and this quickly made hot dressing has a similar flavor.

Use a good quality garlic sausage that has plenty of flavor and is not too fatty. If you do not have Dijon mustard, use any other variety of mild, smooth mustard.

First of all, crush the garlic and put it into a small frying pan with the olive oil. Set them on a medium heat until the garlic sizzles and begins to brown. While the oil is heating up, chop the fennel, core, seed and chop the pepper and cut the slices of sausage into small squares.

As soon as the garlic is ready, stir in the vinegar and mustard. Let the mixture bubble and remove it from the heat.

Divide the fennel, pepper and garlic sausage between four small ramekins or other small dishes. Spoon the hot dressing over the top and garnish with a sprig of parsley.

1 *Heat oil and crushed garlic together until garlic begins to brown.*

2 *Chop fennel and pepper and cut sausage into squares.*

3 *Stir vinegar and mustard into oil and let mixture bubble.*

4 *Divide fennel, pepper and sausage between four small ramekins and spoon dressing over. Garnish with parsley.*

CHICORY AND PEANUTS

Ingredients
½ medium-sized chicory
  (see page 7)
3 oz (75 g) fresh peanuts
2 oz (50 g) raisins
4 Tbs olive oil
2 Tbs white wine vinegar
1 tsp Tabasco sauce
2 Tbs tomato purée

The finely cut, curling leaves of chicory always make exceptionally attractive salads, however large or small. Other names for this delicious salad vegetable are curly chicory or chicoree frisee. You can also use batavia (sometimes called batavian endive) which has less curly and deep-cut leaves but a similar flavor.

The tomato purée and raisins add a richness and sweetness which counteract the freshness and slightly bitter quality of the leaves, and the peanuts add crunch and goodness.

Separate the leaves by cutting them together across the base so that they all fall from the center stem. Divide them between four small plates, arranging them in a nest shape if possible. Put the peanuts and raisins into the center of each nest.

If you have a ready-made oil and vinegar dressing, use 6 tablespoons and beat in the Tabasco sauce and tomato purée. If not, beat the oil and vinegar together first before mixing in the other ingredients.

1 *Separate the leaves by cutting them together across the base.*

2 *Arrange the leaves on four small plates.*

3 *Put the peanuts and raisins in the center.*

4 *After making the dressing, spoon it round the peanuts and raisins.*

GRAPEFRUIT, ORANGE AND SESAME

Ingredients
2 pink grapefruit
2 medium oranges
1 oz (25 g) watercress
5 fl oz (150 ml)
  unsweetened yogurt
2 Tbs tahini (sesame
  paste)
2 Tbs sesame seeds

This is a salad full of contrasts. The two refreshing citrus fruits, one sweet and the other bittersweet, go beautifully with the creamy-textured dressing. Tahini is a paste made from ground sesame seeds. It is always smooth textured and comes in gray or white varieties. The white tahini has the sweeter and creamier flavor. Always stir it before use as the oil separates from the paste on standing.

First hold each fruit on its side and, using a serrated knife, cut off the top and bottom slices of peel and pith. Then hold the fruit upright and cut them off in wide, downwards slices. Halve the fruits lengthwise and cut each half into four crosswise slices.

Arrange four grapefruit and four orange slices on each of four small plates, alternating them in a slightly overlapping line. Insert sprigs of watercress either side of the line of fruit.

Put the tahini into a bowl and gradually beat in the yogurt. Spoon this dressing over the fruits and scatter the sesame seeds over the top.

1 *Cut the peel and pith from the fruit, halve lengthwise and cut each half into four crosswise slices.*

2 *Alternate 4 slices of each fruit on each plate and add watercress either side.*

3 *Beat together the yogurt and tahini and spoon over the fruit. Scatter the sesame seeds on top.*

LIMA BEANS AND GRATED CHEDDAR

Ingredients

6 oz (150 g) lima beans,
  soaked and cooked or,
  15 oz (375 g) canned
  lima beans, drained
8 scallions (salad onions)
3 oz (75 g) Cheddar
  cheese
4 Tbs olive oil
2 Tbs white wine vinegar
1 tsp Worcestershire
  sauce

Lima beans, also called butter beans, take a very long time to cook. If you wish to use home-cooked ones you will need to prepare them in advance and keep them in the refrigerator. You will need 6 oz (150 g) and they should have been soaked in cold water for 8 hours and then simmered for 1½ to 2 hours. Drain, cool and store in a covered plastic container in the refrigerator for no more than two days. However, if you decide at the last minute to make this recipe, canned beans will serve almost as well.

Finely chop the scallions reserving the green tops (also chopped) for garnish. Finely grate the cheese. In a bowl big enough to take all the ingredients, mix together the oil and vinegar (or, if you have a dressing ready made, use 6 tablespoons). Beat in the Worcestershire sauce. Fold in the beans, cheese and chopped scallions.

Divide the salad between four small plates and garnish with the scallion tops.

1 Chop the scallions and grate the cheese.

2 Mix the dressing and fold in all the ingredients except the scallion tops.

3 Divide the salad between four small plates and garnish with the chopped scallion tops.

TUNA FISH AND TOMATO

Ingredients
8 oz (200 g) canned
   tuna fish
4 Tbs unsweetened
   yogurt
½ tsp Tabasco sauce
1 Tbs chopped fennel
   leaves, plus 4 small
   leaves
8 small, firm tomatoes

Tomato salads are always bright and colorful. The creamy-colored tuna makes an ideal contrast in flavor and color, and using yogurt instead of the more usual mayonnaise lightens the flavor.

Use tuna fish that has been canned in oil and not brine, as the oil will be mixed into the salad to become a part of the dressing. The fish has to be flaked for the recipe, so tuna chunks, steaks or flakes may be used.

Use a yogurt that is not too bitter. Fennel is a superb fish herb but, if none is available, you can substitute 3 tablespoons parsley or 2 tablespoons chervil and garnish each plate with a small leaf of the same.

Put the tuna, including the oil, into a bowl and flake it quite finely. Add the yogurt, Tabasco sauce and chopped fennel leaves and mix so they become well incorporated.

Cut each tomato into four crosswise slices and divide them between four small plates. Put a portion of tuna on top and garnish with a fennel leaf.

1 Mix the yogurt, Tabasco sauce and fennel into the flaked tuna.

2 Divide the sliced tomatoes between four small plates.

3 Put the tuna mixture on top and garnish with a fennel leaf.

APPLE, CHEESE AND HAZELNUTS

Ingredients

4 small or 2 large dessert
  apples
6 oz (150 g) cream
  cheese or curd cheese
8 sage leaves, chopped
20 hazelnuts

Either cream cheese or curd cheese is an excellent ingredient in first course salads as its flavor is tangy enough to stimulate the appetite while its creamy texture goes well with salad vegetables and fruits. Combined with herbs it makes an easy dressing.

Use freshly picked hazelnuts when they are available as their crisp, fresh texture and almost milky flavor is unbeatable. Otherwise use ready-shelled nuts.

The dessert apples can be any variety that is crisp and sweet. You will find that the sage in the cheese complements them well. If you are intending to keep the salad standing for a while before it is served, coat the apple slices in fresh lemon juice to prevent them from turning brown.

Shell the nuts, if you are using fresh ones. Quarter and core the apples and cut them into thin lengthwise slices. Arrange the slices round the edge of four small serving plates.

Put the cheese into a bowl and beat in the sage. Put a portion into the center of the apple slices. Halve the nuts and arrange them around the cheese.

1 Quarter, core and thinly slice the apples and arrange round the edge of four small plates.

2 Beat the sage into the cheese.

3 Put the cheese into the center of the plates. Halve the nuts and arrange around the cheese.

2
SIDE SALADS

BELGIAN ENDIVE, BEAN SPROUTS AND TANGERINES

Ingredients
4 small heads of Belgian
   endive (see page 7)
2 oz (50 g) bean sprouts
2 tangerines (or other
   small, soft citrus fruit)
4 Tbs olive oil
2 Tbs cider vinegar
1 tsp clear honey
¼ tsp ginger purée

As this salad has a star-like shape, it is best served on four individual side plates. Use fresh bean sprouts rather than canned as they have a better flavor and crisper texture besides being quicker to use. If tangerines are not available, use clementines, satsumas or other small, soft citrus fruit.

Trim the stalk end from each head of Belgian endive. Once this is done, the leaves are easily separated. Pull them apart and arrange them on each of the side plates with their tips facing outwards. Put a portion of the bean sprouts in the center. Peel the tangerines and cut segments in two lengthwise. Arrange the segments, cut-side up, between the endive and on top of the bean sprouts, using half a fruit per plate.

If you have a ready-made basic oil and vinegar dressing, use 6 tablespoons. If not, beat the oil and vinegar together and then add the honey and ginger purée. Spoon the dressing over the salads, lightly coating the bean sprouts, tangerines and endive.

1 *Arrange endive leaves, tips outwards, on each plate.*

2 *Put a portion of bean sprouts in the center.*

3 *Arrange tangerine segments between the leaves and on top of bean sprouts and spoon dressing over.*

RED LEAF LETTUCE, MUSHROOMS AND GRAPES

Ingredients
2 small red leaf lettuces
4 oz (100 g) button
 mushrooms
24 seedless white grapes
2 Tbs sunflower seeds
4 Tbs olive oil
2 Tbs white wine vinegar
1 tsp white wine flavored
 granular mustard
1 garlic clove, crushed,
 or ¼ tsp garlic purée

Red leaf lettuce, particularly the variety called lollo rosso, is one of the most attractive of salad vegetables, with its red-tinged leaves curling round in frills. Make sure that the mushrooms are white and very fresh with an almost crisp texture. Use 6 tablespoons of the basic oil and vinegar dressing (see page 16) if you have one made up. As an alternative to white wine vinegar, a red wine vinegar or sherry vinegar can be used.

If possible, let the salad stand for 30 minutes before serving, so that the dressing has time to soak into the mushrooms. The salad can either be arranged on four small side plates, or on the side of a cold main dish such as quiche, paté or cold meat.

Trim the ends from the lettuces and separate the leaves. Arrange the leaves on the plates. Thinly slice the mushrooms and put them on top of the lettuce, together with the grapes. Scatter on the sunflower seeds. Beat the remaining ingredients together to make the dressing and spoon it over the salads.

1 *Arrange the lettuce leaves on each of the four plates.*

2 *Put the mushrooms and grapes on the lettuce.*

3 *Scatter on the sunflower seeds and spoon dressing over.*

MIXED LEAF WITH CORN

Ingredients
1 small lettuce
½ small chicory (see
    page 7)
2 oz (50 g) field lettuce
    (lamb's tongue or corn
    salad)
6 scallions (salad onions)
4 Tbs olive oil
2 Tbs white wine vinegar
1 tsp paprika
4 oz (100 g) canned
    corn, drained

The corn in this salad is mixed with the dressing and scattered over the top of a plate of mixed leaves and scallions giving a pleasing, speckled appearance.

Any mixture of salad leaves can be used. Field lettuce is available in both summer and winter. It has small, soft green leaves with rounded ends and a subtle nutty taste. Use a mild-flavored, not bitter, lettuce with loosely packed, tender, green leaves, and the inner, pale leaves of chicory.

Cut the stems from the lettuce and chicory and separate the leaves. Chop the scallions. Arrange the leaves, together with the field lettuce and scallions, in a random fashion on a large serving plate.

If you have some oil and vinegar dressing made up, put 6 tablespoons into a bowl. If not, beat the oil and vinegar together and mix in the paprika and then the corn.

Scatter the corn and dressing over the leaves and scallions.

1 *Prepare the leaves and scallions and arrange on a serving plate.*

2 *Beat together the oil, vinegar and paprika and mix in the corn.*

3 *Scatter corn mixture over the leaves and scallions.*

RADICCHIO LEAVES WITH ARTICHOKE HEARTS AND PEAS

Ingredients
6 oz (150 g) radicchio
10 oz (250 g) canned
   artichoke hearts
8 oz (200 g) canned
   green peas
4 Tbs mayonnaise
4 Tbs chopped parsley
parsley sprigs for
   garnish, optional

In this salad, the leaves of radicchio form cups for a mixture of artichoke hearts and peas in mayonnaise. The red, crisp leaves and the softer-colored and textured salad make a delightful combination.

There are three types of radicchio: the forced, which is the same shape and size as Belgian endive (see page 7); rossa di Treviso, which has open heads streaked with red and cream; and rossa di Verona, which has round, tightly packed, maroon heads. The two latter types are the best for this salad as their leaves are larger than the forced kind.

To separate the leaves of radicchio, cut across the stalk end of the whole head and then pull the leaves apart. Arrange the leaves on a large, flat serving dish. Place the smallest leaves in the center.

Drain the artichoke hearts and chop them. Drain the peas. Put the mayonnaise into a bowl and mix in the parsley and then the artichoke hearts and peas. Spoon the mixture into the cups made by the radicchio leaves.

1 Separate the leaves and arrange on a flat serving plate.

2 Put the mayonnaise into a bowl and mix in the parsley, artichoke hearts and peas.

3 Spoon the mixture into the radicchio leaves.

GREEN SALAD WITH APRICOTS

Ingredients

1 round, firm lettuce
4 Tbs unsweetened
   yogurt
2 Tbs olive oil
1 tsp anchovy paste
2 Tbs chopped tarragon
4 Tbs chopped chives
4 apricots

The anchovy and herb flavorings in this salad give it an eighteenth-century flavor. Anchovy paste can be bought from many specialty food shops and is ideal for use in five-minute salads. It has a strong, salty flavor, so only use small amounts and add no other salt to the dressing. Choose a round, firmly packed, green lettuce, not an iceberg variety as it would not have enough flavor. The apricots added at the end give a contrast in color and a freshness of flavor.

Separate the leaves of the lettuce by cutting across the base and then pulling them apart. Shred them with a sharp knife, holding several leaves in a bundle at a time.

Put the yogurt into a salad bowl and beat in the oil and then the anchovy paste. Mix in the herbs, reserving some chives for garnish, and then fold in the lettuce, making sure it becomes well coated with the dressing.

Halve and pit the apricots and cut them into slices. Scatter them over the top of the salad and garnish with the remaining chives.

1 Separate the lettuce leaves and shred with a sharp knife.

2 In a salad bowl, beat together the yogurt, oil and anchovy paste.

3 Mix in the herbs, reserving some chives, and then the lettuce.

4 Halve, pit and slice the apricots and scatter over the top. Garnish with chives.

CUCUMBER AND TOMATO WITH SOFT CHEESE DRESSING

Ingredients

1 small or ½ large
    cucumber
12 oz (300 g) tomatoes
2 oz (50 g) cream cheese
    or curd cheese
4 Tbs unsweetened
    yogurt
1 garlic clove, crushed,
    or ¼ tsp garlic purée
freshly ground black
    pepper
2 Tbs chopped mint
mint leaves for garnish,
    optional

This is a really fresh-tasting summer salad with a creamy-textured, tangy-flavored dressing and the clean taste of mint. Curd cheese is a light-flavored but creamy-textured medium fat soft cheese. If it is not available, choose another soft cheese that has a similar flavor. Choose a fairly liquid yogurt so that it will thin down the cheese to make a pourable dressing. Use medium-sized tomatoes, ripe but firm and, in late summer, an outdoor-grown cucumber with a sweet, robust flavor.

Wipe the cucumber but do not peel it. Chop it into small cubes. Cut the tomatoes into crosswise slices. Put the cucumber into the center of a flat oval or round serving plate and arrange the tomato slices round the outside.

Cream the cheese in a bowl and beat in the yogurt, garlic, pepper and chopped mint. Spoon the dressing in trails over both the tomatoes and the cucumber. Garnish the salad with whole mint leaves.

1 *Dice the cucumber and slice the tomatoes.*

2 *Put cucumber in center of serving plate with tomato slices around the edge.*

3 *Beat together the cheese, yogurt, garlic, pepper and mint, and spoon over salad.*

WATERCRESS, CARROTS AND PARSLEY

Ingredients

3 oz (75 g) watercress
8 oz (200 g) large
    carrots
6 Tbs chopped parsley
4 Tbs olive oil
2 Tbs white wine vinegar
1 Tbs Worcestershire
    sauce
1 garlic clove, crushed,
    or ¼ teaspoon garlic
    purée

Watercress and carrots are ideal ingredients for winter salads. The watercress needs little preparation. If you buy it in bunches, simply make a cut across the bunch just above the band or tie. If you buy it in bags, there is no need for any preparation at all since the tougher stems have already been removed. Parsley is usually available all year round and its flavor makes a useful addition to the overall blend of ingredients. Worcestershire sauce and cider vinegar add to the robustness of the salad.

Make the dressing first in the bowl in which the salad will be served. Beat together the oil, vinegar, Worcestershire sauce and garlic. Fold in the watercress. Grate the carrots in a food processor or use a hand grater over the bowl so the pieces fall directly onto the watercress. Add the parsley and mix the ingredients together.

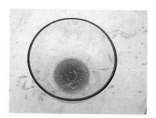

1 In the salad bowl, beat together the oil, vinegar, Worcestershire sauce and garlic.

2 Fold the watercress into the dressing. Grate and add the carrots.

3 Add the parsley and mix ingredients well.

BROWN RICE, LEMON AND ASPARAGUS

Ingredients

8 oz (200 g) brown rice,
  pre-cooked
12 pre-cooked
  asparagus spears or
  12 oz (300 g) canned
  asparagus spears,
  drained
1 lemon
4 Tbs sour cream
1 tsp Dijon mustard
4 Tbs chopped parsley

This is a summer salad of delicate colors and flavors. The flesh of the lemon is used as well as the juice and this gives interesting touches of sharpness amongst the otherwise mild flavors.

Brown rice has a better flavor than white in all dishes and has the added advantage of the grains always remaining separate. Cook it in advance (you should measure the 8 oz (200 g) before cooking, see page 15) and store it in the refrigerator in a covered container for up to two days.

Cut the asparagus spears into 1 in (2.5 cm) lengths. Cut the lemon in half. Squeeze the juice from one half. Put the other half on a chopping board, cut-side down, and cut off all the peel and pith. Finely dice the flesh, removing all the pits and saving as much juice as possible.

Put the sour cream into a salad bowl. Beat in the lemon juice and the Dijon mustard. Mix in the rice, asparagus, chopped lemon and parsley.

1 Cut the asparagus into 1 in (2.5 cm) lengths

2 Squeeze the juice from one half of the lemon. Chop the flesh only of the other.

3 In a salad bowl, beat together the sour cream, lemon juice and Dijon mustard.

4 Mix in the rice, asparagus, parsley and chopped lemon flesh.

CHINESE CABBAGE AND GREEN PEPPERS

Ingredients
½ Chinese cabbage
2 green peppers
4 Tbs sesame oil or
  olive oil
2 Tbs cider vinegar
1 Tbs soy sauce
1 tsp tahini (sesame
  paste)
1 garlic clove, crushed,
  or ¼ teaspoon garlic
  purée

The Chinese cabbage and soy sauce give this salad an oriental flavor. Chinese cabbage, also called Chinese leaves, has large, densely packed heads and half a small head will be quite enough for four people. Bittersweet green peppers and a rich dressing make contrasts in color and flavor.

Sesame oil has a rich nutty flavor and combines well with soy sauce. Olive oil may be used as a substitute and white wine vinegar can replace the cider vinegar.

Tahini is also a product of the sesame seed and takes the form of a thick paste. Use either the light or dark variety and stir it before use if it has become separated.

Cut the half cabbage lengthwise in two and shred each piece, removing any tough core that may be at the base. Core, seed and dice the peppers.

In a salad bowl, beat together the oil, vinegar, soy sauce, tahini and garlic and fold in the Chinese cabbage and green peppers.

1 *Halve cabbage lengthwise and shred.*

2 *Core, seed and dice the peppers.*

3 *Beat oil, vinegar, soy sauce, tahini and garlic and fold in cabbage and peppers.*

3
SALADS FOR A
MAIN MEAL

CHICKEN AND RED PEPPERS

Ingredients
4 Tbs mayonnaise
4 Tbs unsweetened
  yogurt
1 tsp paprika
¼ tsp Tabasco sauce
1 Tbs tomato purée
4 cooked chicken breasts
2 Tbs chopped basil
2 red peppers
edible flowers – e.g.
  nasturtiums, pansies
  (if available)

This is a colorful summer salad with crisp, sharp-tasting red peppers providing a fresh contrast to the creamy-textured dressing. Use edible flowers if you have them to make the salad look stunning. The chicken has to be cooked beforehand – the instructions for this are given on page 14. Use breasts rather than legs or drumsticks as they can be quickly cut into cubes. For serving, choose a large, oval platter that looks good in the center of the table, or decorate dinner plates with individual servings.

In a fairly large bowl, big enough to take the diced chicken, beat together the mayonnaise, yogurt, paprika, Tabasco sauce and tomato purée. Dice the chicken breasts and fold them into the dressing, together with the basil.

Core the peppers and cut them thinly in rounds. Arrange them overlapping around the outside of each individual plate, or of your main serving plate. Put the chicken mixture in a mound in the middle of the plate and decorate with edible flowers.

1 Beat together the mayonnaise, yogurt, paprika, Tabasco sauce and tomato purée.

2 Fold in the diced chicken and chopped basil.

3 Arrange the peppers round the edge of the plate.

4 Scoop chicken onto the center of the plate and decorate with edible flowers.

SAUSAGE SALAD

Ingredients

1 lb sausages,
   pre-cooked
4 Tbs mayonnaise
4 Tbs unsweetened
   yogurt
2 tsp preserved grated
   horseradish
¼ tsp mustard powder
2 small heads of lettuce
   with tightly packed
   leaves
6 tomatoes
4 small, cooked beets
   (beetroot)
alfalfa sprouts or
   mustard and cress

This is a good, hearty salad that is excellent served with baked potatoes. Reheating sausages takes only a small amount of time and adds a special touch to the salad, their rich juiciness contrasting well with the lettuce and tomato. The sausages can be baked, grilled or fried in advance and left to go cold.

Choose heads of lettuce that are small and tightly packed, with a good proportion of dark green leaves and a strong flavor which suits the other ingredients.

Put the sausages under a high grill (preheating is not necessary if they are already cooked) and leave them for 3 minutes, turning once. Meanwhile, in a large bowl, mix together the mayonnaise, yogurt, horseradish and mustard powder. Shred the lettuce, chop the tomatoes and thinly slice the beets. Mix the lettuce and tomatoes into the dressing. Take the sausages from under the grill, slice them and mix them into the salad.

Either pile the salad onto one large serving plate or divide it between four individual dinner plates. Arrange the beets round the edge. Scatter alfalfa sprouts or mustard and cress over the top.

1 *Put the sausages under the grill to heat through.*

2 *Mix together the mayonnaise, yogurt, horseradish and mustard powder.*

3 *Shred lettuce, chop tomatoes, slice sausages and mix into dressing.*

4 *Put the salad onto a serving plate. Surround with slices of beets and scatter alfalfa or cress over the top.*

Avocados topped with ham

Ingredients

4 avocados
2 Tbs cider vinegar
4 Tbs olive oil
1 tsp spiced granular
    mustard
6 oz (150 g) cooked
    lean ham
12 sage leaves

Avocados are an easily prepared and substantial raw ingredient for a main course salad. Choose large ones that are ripe but still firm, so that the flesh is soft and butter-textured and a good green color.

The best ham for this recipe is home cooked (see page 14). Cut it into slices about ¼ inch (6 mm) thick. If you would rather buy the ham, look out for the type that has been cooked on the bone and is cut to order. Thin slices of ham in vacuum packs do not taste as good.

Most spiced granular mustards go well with ham, but those made with honey or cider are best of all.

Put the vinegar into a bowl that is big enough to hold the ham when it is diced. Halve and pit the avocados and brush the cut surfaces with a little of the vinegar. This will prevent them from going brown.

Add the oil and mustard to the vinegar and beat well. Finely dice the ham and finely chop four of the sage leaves. Mix them both into the dressing.

Pile the ham mixture into and on top of the avocado halves. Garnish each avocado half with a whole sage leaf.

1 *Halve and pit the avocados and brush with vinegar.*

2 *Beat the oil and mustard into the vinegar, and add the diced ham and chopped sage.*

3 *Pile the ham onto the avocados and garnish with sage leaves.*

CURRIED CHICKPEAS AND ALMONDS

Ingredients

6 Tbs unsweetened
  yogurt
2 Tbs olive oil
¼ tsp curry paste
1 tsp turmeric
1 garlic clove, crushed
8 oz (200 g) chickpeas,
  soaked and cooked or
  16 oz (400 g) canned
  chickpeas, drained
4 oz (100 g) almonds
2 oz (50 g) raisins
leaves of lettuce or other
  leafy salad vegetable
4 Tbs chopped fresh
  coriander
warmed pita breads

Both chickpeas and almonds suit curry flavors and the soft texture of one and the crunchy texture of the other go well together. The raisins add a sweet contrast and the green leaves a touch of freshness and a brighter color.

If you are using home-cooked chickpeas, they must have been soaked for 2 hours and then simmered for a further 2 hours and drained. They will keep covered in the refrigerator for two days.

Curry pastes vary in hotness and flavor so use one that suits your taste. Use unskinned almonds as they have more flavor and moisture than blanched. For lining the bowls choose whichever leafy vegetables are available.

Put the yogurt into a large bowl and gradually beat in the olive oil. Add the curry paste, turmeric and garlic and beat well again. Fold in the chickpeas, almonds and raisins. Line four large, individual bowls with the leaves and pile the chickpeas, almonds and raisins inside. Scatter coriander on top.

1 *Beat together the yogurt, oil, curry paste, turmeric and garlic.*

2 *Fold in the chickpeas, almonds and raisins.*

3 *Line four bowls with salad leaves. Pile salad in center and scatter coriander on top.*

EGG, SHRIMP AND CRAB

Ingredients

6 oz (150 g) alfalfa
   sprouts or 4 boxes
   mustard and cress
4 eggs (hard boiled)
8 oz (200 g) shrimp
8 oz (200 g) crab meat,
   canned or frozen
20 cherry tomatoes
3 fl oz (75 ml)
   mayonnaise
1 tsp paprika
pinch cayenne pepper
1 dill pickle (pickled dill
   cucumber)
parsley sprigs for garnish

This is a classic seafood salad using ingredients that require little or no preparation. The cherry tomatoes need a quick rinse under cold water and you must remember to boil the eggs in advance. They will keep, unpeeled, in cold water for a few hours, or in the refrigerator for one day. Home-made mayonnaise is best (see page 17).

The salad is prepared and served on individual plates. Arrange the alfalfa or mustard and cress in a circle round the edge of each plate, leaves pointing outwards. Peel the eggs and cut them in half lengthwise. Put an egg half, cut-side down, on opposite sides of each plate. To either side of the eggs, place a portion of shrimp and a portion of crab, leaving room in the center for the mayonnaise. Slice the tomatoes and arrange them in a circle around the eggs, shrimp and crab.

Put the mayonnaise into a bowl and mix in the paprika and cayenne pepper. Finely chop the dill pickle and mix it into the mayonnaise. Spoon the mayonnaise into the center of each plate and garnish with a sprig of parsley.

1 *Arrange the alfalfa or mustard and cress in a circle around the edge of four individual plates*

2 *Peel the eggs, cut them in half lengthwise and put 2 halves on opposite sides of each plate.*

3 *Put portions of shrimp and crab meat either side of the eggs, leaving a small space in the center.*

4 *Mix the paprika, cayenne pepper and chopped pickle into the mayonnaise and spoon into the center.*

BLUE CHEESE, WATERCRESS AND WALNUTS

Ingredients
4 Tbs olive oil
2 Tbs white wine vinegar
¼ tsp cayenne pepper
1 garlic clove, crushed
6 oz (150 g) watercress
6 oz (150 g) mild blue
  cheese
4 oz (100 g) walnuts
8 tomatoes
8 walnut halves

This is a salad of bright colors and strong flavors that is good on autumn and winter evenings.

Choose watercress with plenty of large leaves and tomatoes that are ripe but firm. The cheese should be soft but firm enough to be cut into cubes. If you are lucky enough to be able to buy fresh or 'wet' walnuts, and have the time to shell enough to make up the required amount for the recipe, then do so. It will be worth it for their crisp texture.

In a large bowl, beat together the oil, vinegar, cayenne pepper and garlic; or, if you have a ready-made oil and vinegar mixture, shake it and use 6 tablespoons with the cayenne and garlic.

Chop the watercress, using the stalks as well as the leaves. Finely dice the cheese and chop the walnuts. Fold the watercress into the dressing and then carefully mix in the cheese and walnuts.

Divide the salad between four dinner plates. Slice the tomatoes and arrange the slices around the salads. Garnish each salad with 2 walnut halves.

1 *Beat together the oil, vinegar, cayenne and garlic.*

2 *Chop the watercress, cheese and walnuts and fold into dressing.*

3 *Put the salad onto plates. Garnish with tomato slices and walnut halves.*

Beans and Feta Cheese

Ingredients

12 oz (300 g) shelled
fava or broad beans,
cooked, or 12 oz (300 g)
canned broad beans
8 oz (200 g) flageolet
beans, soaked and
cooked, or 16 oz
(400 g) canned
flageolet beans
1 lemon
4 Tbs olive oil
pinch cayenne pepper
2 Tbs chopped fennel
leaves
2 Tbs chopped mint
2 scallions (salad
onions), finely chopped
6 oz (150 g) feta cheese

This is a salad of soft greens, dotted with the darker green of the summer herbs and scallions. Both the beans have very mild, soft flavors which provide a good contrast to the tangy saltiness of the feta cheese. The lemon juice adds a touch of sharpness.

If you are using fresh broad beans, cook them in advance for 10 minutes in lightly salted boiling water. Drain and cool them and store in a covered container in the refrigerator for 2 days. The flageolet beans should be soaked for 2 hours and cooked for 1 hour 30 minutes, then drained, cooled and stored in the same way as the broad beans. The two types of tinned beans should simply be drained.

Squeeze the juice from half the lemon into a bowl. Beat in the oil and cayenne pepper. Fold in the beans. Dice the feta cheese and mix it into the salad together with the herbs and chopped scallions.

Pile the salad into the center of a flat serving plate. Cut four thin slices from the remaining lemon half. If you wish, make a cut in each slice from the center to the edge and make the slices into twists. Put these or plain lemon slices on top of the salad.

1 *In a bowl, beat together the lemon juice, oil and cayenne pepper.*

2 *Dice the cheese and fold into the beans, together with chopped herbs and scallions.*

3 *Cut the remaining lemon half into slices and make into twists if you wish, to use as garnish.*

4 *Pile the salad onto a serving plate and garnish with lemon.*

BULGUR WHEAT AND TUNA FISH

Ingredients

8 oz (200 g) bulgur
   wheat
8 oz (200 g) canned
   tuna fish
4 tomatoes
6 scallions (salad onions)
6 green olives, pitted
4 Tbs olive oil
juice ½ lemon
freshly ground black
   pepper
4 Tbs chopped parsley
parsley sprigs for garnish

This is an easy-to-make and easy-to-eat salad that is a complete meal in itself. Serve it in bowls and eat it with forks or spoons for a quick and easy lunch.

Bulgur wheat is a pre-cooked grain which is quickly softened by pouring boiling water onto it. Choose tuna fish that is canned in oil rather than brine as it has a more succulent flavor.

Put the bulgur wheat into a bowl and pour in boiling water to cover it. Leave it to soak while you prepare the rest of the ingredients.

Drain the tuna. Chop the tomatoes and scallions and halve the olives. In a bowl big enough to take all the ingredients, beat together the oil, lemon juice and pepper.

Drain the bulgur wheat in a sieve, run cold water through it and drain again. Squeeze to remove any excess moisture. Mix the wheat into the salad dressing. Add the tuna, flaking it as you remove it from the can, and then the tomatoes, scallions and parsley.

To serve, divide the salad between four bowls and garnish with the parsley sprigs.

1 *Pour boiling water on wheat and leave to soak. Drain tuna, chop tomatoes and scallions and halve olives.*

2 *Beat the oil, lemon juice and pepper in a bowl.*

3 *Drain wheat, run cold water through and squeeze dry.*

4 *Mix the wheat, tuna, tomatoes, scallions and parsley into the dressing.*

OYSTERS AND ORANGES

Ingredients

2 dozen opened oysters
2 sweet red or yellow
  peppers
2 large oranges
3 Tbs olive oil
1 tsp paprika
2 Tbs chopped parsley
1 cucumber

Fresh oysters make wonderful salads and as long as you have them opened by the person selling them to you they need no preparation apart from a quick cutting from their shells. If you are using frozen oysters, allow one hour at room temperature for them to thaw out. Canned oysters can also be used but their flavor is not as fine.

Squeeze the juice from one of the oranges and put it into a large bowl. Beat in the olive oil and the paprika. Cut the peel and pith from the remaining orange. Cut the flesh into lengthwise quarters and slice thinly. Core and seed the peppers and cut them into julienne strips. Mix the orange and peppers into the dressing.

The oysters are attached to their shells by a small piece of muscle on their underside. Loosen this with your finger or small, round-bladed knife and tip the oyster straight into the salad. Add the parsley and mix the ingredients together.

Pile the salad into the center of a large serving plate. Cut the cucumber into thin slices and arrange them around the edge.

1 *Squeeze the juice from one orange and mix with the oil and paprika in a large bowl.*

2 *Add orange and pepper slices to the dressing and fold in oysters and parsley.*

3 *Pile salad onto serving plate and surround with cucumber slices.*

4
HOT SALADS

Hot carrots with capers

Ingredients
2 Tbs white wine vinegar
2 tsp Dijon mustard
1 Tbs chopped capers
and some whole for
garnish
2 Tbs chopped parsley
4 Tbs olive oil
12 oz (300 g) carrots

This is a crisp winter salad which goes well with plainly cooked meat dishes and can also provide a delicious contrast in flavor to milder tasting vegetarian meals. The carrots maintain a crisp, crunchy texture and the addition of the vinegar and capers gives a sharp, salad flavor.

The trick in the swiftness of preparation is that only one main ingredient is used and it is quickly prepared while the oil is heating up. Use long carrots, if possible. You will find them easier to slice.

In a small bowl, beat together the vinegar and mustard. Mix in the chopped capers and parsley. Put the oil into a large frying pan or wok and set it on a high heat. Slice the carrots thinly while the oil is heating.

Put the carrots into the hot oil and stir them around for 1 minute. Pour in the vinegar mixture and let it boil until it has reduced almost completely. Tip the salad and any remaining dressing into a serving dish, garnish with whole capers and take it to the table as soon as possible.

1 *Beat together the vinegar and mustard and add chopped capers and parsley.*

2 *While oil is heating, slice the carrots.*

3 *Stir carrots in the hot oil for 1 minute.*

4 *Add vinegar mixture and let it reduce almost completely.*

HOT BEETS WITH HORSERADISH

Ingredients
2 Tbs olive oil
1 lb (400 g) cooked beets
  (beetroot), peeled
6 scallions (salad onions)
1 Tbs white wine vinegar
6 Tbs sour cream
¼ tsp mustard powder
2 Tbs preserved grated
  horseradish

Beets and horseradish are both ingredients that go
well with beef and also with cheese dishes.

Use home-cooked beets if possible. If you are
buying canned beets, they must not be preserved in
vinegar or acetic acid as this would spoil the mild
flavor of the vegetable that goes so well with the
sharp dressing.

Put the oil into a large frying pan and set it on a
medium heat. While it is heating, cut the beets into
¼ inch (6 mm) thick slices and finely chop the
scallions. Put the beets into the pan and cook,
turning frequently, for 1 minute, or until they have
heated through. Transfer the beets to a large, flat
serving plate.

Stir the vinegar, sour cream, mustard powder and
grated horseradish into the pan. Let the mixture
bubble and spoon it over the beets. Scatter the
chopped scallions over the salad.

1 *Set oil on medium heat.
Slice the beets and chop the
scallions.*

2 *Put beets into pan, heat
through for 1 minute and
remove to serving plate.*

3 *Stir vinegar, sour cream,
mustard powder and
horseradish into pan.
Heat through.*

4 *Spoon dressing over
beets and scatter the
chopped scallions.*

HOT PEACHES WITH LETTUCE

Ingredients

2 small, tightly packed
    green lettuces
4 small peaches
3 Tbs olive oil
1 garlic clove
3 Tbs chopped fennel
    leaves
juice 1 lemon
3 Tbs sour cream
4 small fennel sprigs for
    garnish

This sharp-sweet salad with its contrasting textures of crisp and melting and its creamy dressing is excellent with cold chicken or turkey and with vegetarian quiches.

Cut the lettuces crosswise into slices about ¾ inch (2 cm) thick. To prepare the peaches, use a small, sharp knife and cut them in a circle from top to bottom following the groove in the fruit. Pull the two halves apart and pull away the pit.

Put the oil into a frying pan or wok and set it on a moderate heat. Cut the garlic into it while it is heating up. Put in the lettuce, peaches and chopped fennel and stir them in the hot oil for 30 seconds or until you can see the lettuce just beginning to soften. Take care not to overcook it or it may become wilted in texture. Pour in the lemon juice and bring it to the boil. Stir in 2 tablespoons of the cream and let it bubble.

Immediately put the salad into four individual bowls and garnish each one with a dollop of cream and a small fennel sprig.

1 Cut lettuces into ¾ inch (2 cm) thick slices. Pit and slice peaches.

2 Heat oil in frying pan on moderate heat and chop in garlic.

3 Put in lettuce, peaches and fennel and stir for 30 seconds.

4 Pour in lemon juice, boil and stir in sour cream. When it bubbles, remove salad from heat and transfer to individual bowls.

HOT CABBAGE AND PINEAPPLE

Ingredients

1 small green cabbage
4 celery sticks
4 Tbs olive oil
1 garlic clove
2 thick slices fresh
  pineapple
1 oz (25 g) shelled
  walnuts
2 Tbs lemon vinegar
  (page 16) or white
  wine vinegar

Pineapple, cabbage and celery make a salad of soft green and yellow colors. The cabbage and celery remain light and crisp while the pineapple adds a soft, juicy contrast and the walnuts add richness. The salad goes beautifully with all cold meats and also with pasta and vegetarian bean dishes.

Use a green cabbage that has a crisp texture and is not too densely packed. Fresh pineapple obviously works best but, if none is available, you can substitute 2 slices of pineapple that has been canned in fruit juice rather than syrup.

Shred the cabbage and chop the celery. Heat the oil in a large frying pan or wok on a high heat and, while it is heating, chop in the garlic. Mix in the cabbage and celery and stir-fry them for 2 minutes. Between stirring, take the whole pineapple and cut away a slice from the stalk end. Cut two thick slices from the fruit. Cut away the edges and cores from these slices and chop the flesh. Chop the walnuts.

Mix the pineapple and walnuts into the cabbage and celery. Pour in the vinegar and let it bubble. Take from the heat and serve as soon as possible.

1 *Shred the cabbage and celery.*

2 *Heat the oil with the garlic, add cabbage and celery and stir-fry for 2 minutes.*

3 *Add pineapple slices, chopped walnuts and vinegar and let bubble.*

HOT MUSHROOMS, PARSLEY AND CASHEW NUTS

Ingredients
8 oz (200 g) button
  mushrooms
1 oz (25 g) parsley
4 Tbs olive oil
1 garlic clove
2 Tbs white wine vinegar
1 tsp Worcestershire
  sauce
2 oz (50 g) cashew nut
  pieces
parsley sprigs for
  garnish, optional

This salad is small but substantial and is ideal served either as an accompaniment to a light main meal or as a first course.

Using parsley as a main ingredient rather than a small flavoring adds both color and flavor to the salad. You will find large sprigs tied in a bunch quicker to chop than small vacuum-packed sprigs. The mushrooms should be white and fresh.

Thinly slice the mushrooms and chop the parsley. Put the oil into a large frying pan. Set it on a high heat and chop in the garlic. While the oil is heating, mix together the vinegar and Worcestershire sauce.

Put the mushrooms and cashew nut pieces into the oil and stir them for 1 minute. Mix in the parsley. Pour in the vinegar mixture and let it bubble. Take the pan from the heat.

To serve as an accompaniment to a main meal, put the salad into one serving bowl. To serve it as a first course, put it into individual bowls. It can be garnished with small parsley sprigs if wished.

1 *Thinly slice mushrooms and chop parsley.*

2 *Heat oil and garlic and mix together vinegar and Worcestershire sauce.*

3 *Put mushrooms and cashew nuts into oil and stir-fry for 1 minute.*

4 *Mix in parsley and then the vinegar mixture, and let bubble.*

INDEX